T0390332

THE HIDDEN HEROES OF SCIENCE

Written by
PETER GALLIVAN

Illustrated by
ROBBIE CATHRO

DK | Penguin Random House

Author Peter Gallivan
Illustrator Robbie Cathro

Editor Becca Arlington
US Senior Editor Shannon Beatty
Americanization Editor Lori Cates Hand
Project Art Editor Sonny Flynn
Designer Brandie Tully-Scott
Proofreaders Thomas Mantell, Anna Bonnerjea
Sensitivity Readers Lisa Davis, Dee Hudson
Jacket Coordinator Elin Woosnam
Managing Art Editor Elle Ward
Senior Production Editor Nikoleta Parasaki
Senior Production Controller Leanne Burke
Publisher James Mitchem

First American Edition, 2025
Published in the United States by DK Publishing,
a division of Penguin Random House LLC
1745 Broadway, 20th Floor, New York, NY 10019

Published in Great Britain in 2025 by Dorling Kindersley Ltd.
in association with the Royal Institution of Great Britain.
Registered charity no. 227938

ISBN: 978-0-5939-6906-9

Printed and bound in Slovakia

www.dk.com

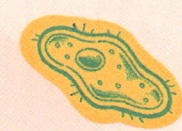

THE HIDDEN HEROES OF SCIENCE

CONTENTS

What is science?

Before we start meeting some scientists, it's important to understand what exactly a scientist is! Even though they all do very different things—from looking at distant planets to looking for new animals in the jungle—there are still things scientists all have in common...

Questioning things

Scientists come up with ideas to explain why things are the way they are. They look at the world in detail and suggest explanations for why it could be that way.

Experimenting

To really understand if their ideas are correct, scientists do experiments. They measure things in detail, make changes, and see if their ideas hold up.

Solving problems

Many scientists work to help make the world a better place. This might be by finding new medicines to treat diseases, or by helping protect animals that are going extinct.

The first scientist?

It's hard to really say exactly who the first scientist was—in fact, you could say that the very first humans to walk the earth over 100,000 years ago were scientists. They explored their environment, made tools and equipment to make their lives easier, and generally tried to make sense of planet earth and the vastness of the universe above them.

We only really know if people in the past were doing "science" if they left behind evidence. Although we have found amazing cave paintings made by these long-distant early human ancestors, we need to go a little further forward in time to meet our first scientists...

Imhotep
Building the foundations

The first scientist in this book lived in ancient Egypt, a civilization that started around five thousand years ago. You might think it would be impossible to know anything about people who lived so long ago, but the Egyptians had a secret weapon up their sleeves: writing.

Writing it down

At the time of the ancient Egyptians, writing things down had been around for only a few hundred years, so just a few people could read and write. But these scribes wrote down almost everything that happened in society, giving us an amazingly detailed picture of life in ancient Egypt. Some scribes were in charge of the market, recording money and food changing hands. Others were in charge of armies, making sure they had enough supplies to fight.

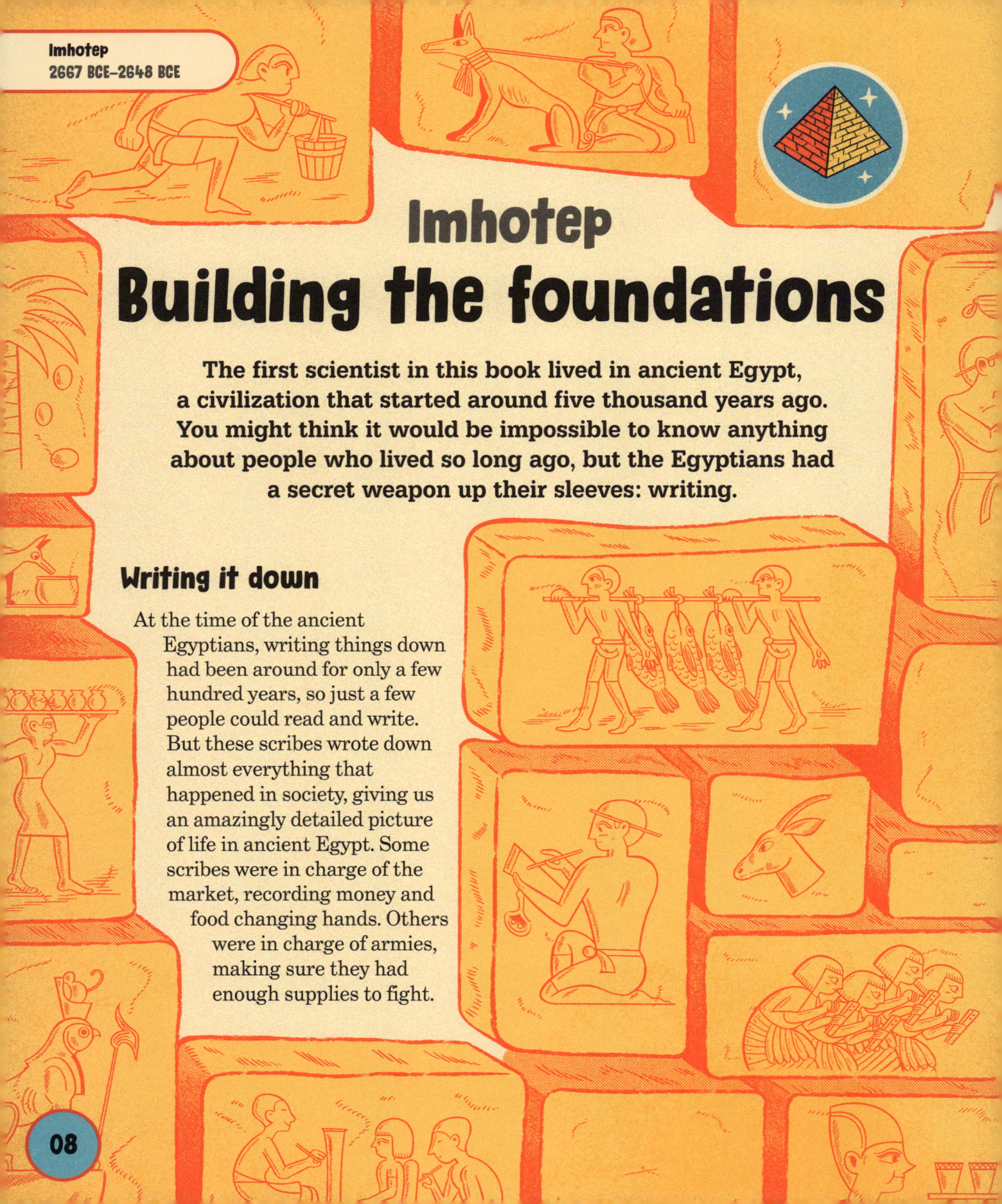

Towering achievements

Perhaps the greatest scribe who lived was a man called Imhotep. Due to his talent with numbers, Imhotep was in charge of designing and constructing buildings for the ruling king, Djoser. Today, we call someone who designs a building an architect, and this job involves a lot of science! They need to understand how different materials can be used in a building to make sure it will be strong and not collapse when it's finished.

The largest buildings in ancient Egypt were burial tombs for the kings. Because Imhotep excelled at designing buildings, he was promoted to chief architect, and tasked with the biggest job of his life—designing a lavish tomb for the king, taller and more memorable than all others before it.

FUN FACT

Imhotep was also one of the first doctors in the world! He realized that illness was just a natural part of life and not caused by a curse from ancient gods.

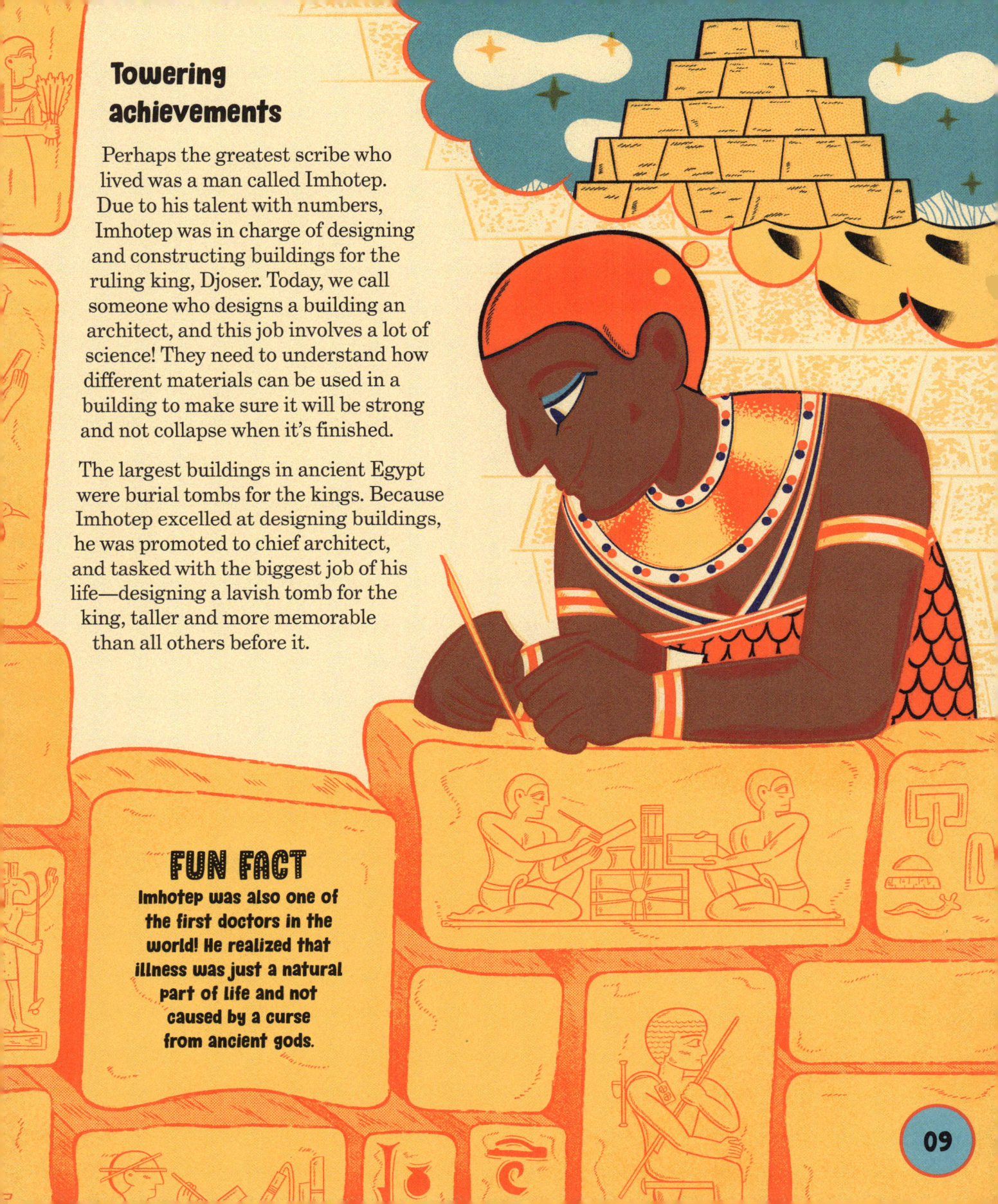

Building tall

At the time, most burial tombs were low, blocky buildings. By stacking up six of these on top of each other, each smaller than the last, Imhotep created a tall but stable building. He used blocks of stone, rather than bricks made from mud, to create a long-lasting building. And he was certainly right: this first pyramid he built reached an amazing 200 ft (61 m) tall and still stands today, almost 5,000 years later!

King Djoser was so impressed with his pyramid that he wrote Imhotep's name alongside his own on the pyramid, something unheard of at the time.

Inspired by Imhotep's innovative design, future scribes went on to design even greater pyramids. One hundred years later, the tallest pyramid ever was built, the famous Great Pyramid of Giza. At 482 ft (147 m), it remained the tallest human-made structure in the world for more than 3,800 years!

Imhotep's influence was so great that, even when the ancient Greeks conquered ancient Egypt, they built temples dedicated to him.

Changing the world

Imhotep inspired scribes for thousands of years, but faded from memory as other impressive buildings were built across the world. However, the amazing skyscrapers we see reaching toward the sky today owe their inspiration to Imhotep and may be gone in a few hundred years, while the solid stone pyramids will stand regardless.

Hypatia
Leader of thought

Scientific thinking started in ancient Egypt and soon spread throughout Europe, the Middle East, and Asia. The ancient Greeks, however, really kicked things into overdrive. Where the Egyptians were practical thinkers, the Greeks went even deeper, using the power of a seemingly simple word: "why."

Thinking it through

The ancient Greeks pioneered a new way of thinking that we now call philosophy. Philosophers are people who try to understand why things are the way they are—the first step of the modern scientific method.

Great cities were built around the Mediterranean Sea, containing some of the first universities and libraries in the world. It was here that philosophers did their work, spending hours sitting around thinking, and discussing their ideas with others—not a bad life, really! They summarized their thoughts into theories, attempting to explain everything they could see in the world.

Ancient philosophers studied music alongside math, believing harmonious music showed the purity of math.

What about women?

Unfortunately, most of the famous philosophers you might have heard of—Plato, Socrates, Aristotle—are all men. There were, however, some women who went against the grain and made a big impact in this male-dominated world. Hypatia was born in the city of Alexandria in Egypt, one of the great centers of learning in the Roman Empire. This city followed the example set by the ancient Greeks, and was home to many famous philosophers.

Hypatia's father was an important mathematician at a university, and taught his daughter himself, while most other girls had to stay home and help around the house. This allowed Hypatia to learn in the Great Library of Alexandria. This was one of the largest libraries in the world at its time, containing thousands of books from ancient philosophers of the last thousand years. By the time she was an adult, Hypatia had surpassed her father as a mathematician and thinker, and took over his position as head of the university.

Studying and teaching

Hypatia improved lots of ancient Greek mathematics, building and improving on the work that came before her. She also developed the astrolabe—the first mechanical device that could accurately track the movements of stars and planets in the sky.

The most important thing Hypatia did, however, was teach others. She regularly gave lectures to the public in Alexandria, helping everyday people understand the work of the great philosophers before her. These were very popular events, with people traveling from across the Roman Empire to hear her. Her teachings explored the idea that numbers are a universal language that can be used to understand how the world works.

Hypatia died just before the collapse of the Roman Empire, making her one of the last Greek philosophers.

An education for everyone

Hypatia helped make her city of Alexandria a welcoming and diverse place where more people were able to learn. She showed how important education is—it is useful not only to think up new theories, but also to help others understand these ideas. Even more importantly, she helped show that women could be just as smart thinkers as men!

Abbas ibn Firnas
Science takes flight!

How much do you trust in science? Would you be prepared to risk your life to show you were right? Our next hero took an amazing leap of faith to prove his ideas were correct, propelling the world of science forward in the process.

Learning by doing

Abbas ibn Firnas was born in the city of Cordoba, Spain. In the 800s, Spain was part of a large region of Islamic rule. This region stretched from Afghanistan, through the Middle East, North Africa, most of Spain, and all the way to Portugal.

Cordoba was a great center of learning, home to many amazing scientists and thinkers. This was a groundbreaking time for scientific discovery, and a huge amount of knowledge we still use today comes from this Islamic period.

Learning everything

From a young age, Abbas was interested in science—he would take things apart and piece them back together, to figure out how they worked. He gained an extensive education, learning math, astronomy, music, poetry, and art.

Abbas built a clock powered by water and a giant planetarium—a scale model of the solar system, with planets orbiting the sun. His greatest invention, however, was thanks to someone else's bad luck. In 852, a brave inventor named Armen Firman attempted to fly like a bird, using a cape he had designed to help. After leaping into the air, Armen soon sped back down to earth, his life saved only by his cape working like a parachute to slow his fall.

FUN FACT

Engineers today still use birds as inspiration for plane design. The end of most wings curl up, which makes them more efficient—a design copied from eagles!

17

Reaching for the sky

The flying experiment was a spectacular failure for Armen, but immediately Abbas focused on building a successful flying machine. He observed the golden eagles that flew above his city, studying the shapes of their wings and how they moved. After 20 years of work, his invention was ready: two large wings, covered in silk and eagle feathers.

Abbas was 70 years old when the day finally came to test his invention. He hiked to the top of a nearby mountain, and said to a friend, "If all goes well, after soaring for a time, I should return safely to your side." Thankfully this prediction was correct! Abbas stayed in the air for about 10 minutes, slowly gliding to the ground. This was the first time in history a human had ever flown.

FUN FACT
Abbas ibn Firnas also invented reading glasses. He created a "reading stone"—a shaped piece of glass that could magnify written text.

To honor his contribution to flight, a crater on the moon was named after Abbas ibn Firnas.

Leaving a legacy

Unfortunately, a bumpy landing injured Abbas's back, and this was the only flight he ever made. He spent the rest of his days writing down more of his ideas, for others to develop in the future.

Today, most people think of the Wright brothers, who made the first flight with a powered machine in 1903, as the inventors of aviation. But we shouldn't forget brave Abbas ibn Firnas, who was so confident in science that he leapt off a mountain in his flying machine, over a thousand years before.

Ibn al-Haytham
The first experimenter

In the city of Basra, Iraq, multi-talented scientist, writer of over 200 books, and inventor Ibn al-Haytham made many amazing discoveries. One of these was how our eyes work...

Making a method

At the time, it was believed we could see because light shone out of our eyes and onto objects—a theory developed around 300 BCE. Ibn al-Haytham explained instead that light shines from objects, such as the sun, and reflects off other objects into our eyes.

But it was the way Ibn al-Haytham made this discovery that was significant. At the time, most scientists would make observations and come up with theories to explain what they saw.

Ibn al-Haytham, however, went one step further: he built his own equipment so that he could perform experiments and carefully test whether his theories were actually correct.

This process is what we today call the scientific method. It is now the procedure all scientists use to prove that their ideas are correct (or not!). So we can basically thank Ibn al-Haytham that we know anything at all!

Although Ibn al-Haytham invented the way we do science, the word "scientist" was actually invented much later, in 1834!

FUN FACT
Ibn al-Haytham's books were translated from Arabic into Latin, and were read by scientists hundreds of years later.

Maria Merian
A flowering of science

Maria Merian's parents were artists, and she too was a talented painter. As a child, she loved to collect insects and flowers and spend hours drawing detailed images of them. Just like her parents, she became employed as a painter, and sold books filled with her amazing paintings of flowers.

Ideas out of the mud

As much as she loved creating images of flowers, Maria's favorite things to draw were caterpillars. She kept them as pets, drawing them as they grew, and writing down her observations. At this time, many scientists thought that insects magically came to life from the mud. Some even published "recipes" to make flies or bees using raw meat or honey!

But Maria knew this was not true. Thanks to her careful observations, she knew instead that caterpillars began life as tiny eggs, hatched into caterpillars, and formed pupae, before eventually emerging as adult butterflies, ready to lay eggs and start the cycle again. Maria published her paintings with detailed notes in a groundbreaking book called *The Wondrous Transformation of Caterpillars*. Her detailed paintings showed the life cycles of these insects alongside the plants they fed on, proving her observations to be correct.

FUN FACT

Maria was one of the first scientists to write about the Surinam toad. Her paintings show their unusual behavior: babies are born from holes inside their mothers' backs!

A number of species have been named after Maria, including eight different caterpillars.

Travels to the land of the caterpillar

At this time, Maria lived in Amsterdam, the Netherlands, and every day boats would arrive filled with natural wonders from far away. Maria marveled at the tropical plants and insects, but longed to see these animals alive herself. So, in 1699, she sold everything she owned to fund a two-month journey by boat to Suriname, in South America.

Maria was likely the first person to travel across the vast Atlantic Ocean to study the animals of South America. She had only her daughter for company. What they found in Suriname was more than Maria could have possibly imagined. She got to work drawing all the amazing wildlife, learning quickly that tropical jungles had insects much more dangerous than in Amsterdam!

Bringing nature to life

Unfortunately, Maria became ill and returned home after two years. The books of her paintings made in Suriname were instant hits, and showed an amazing array of wildlife never before seen by people in Europe. Her detailed paintings showed animals in the wild, from leafcutter ants forming bridges with their bodies, to giant tarantulas devouring birds.

Maria's paintings each took a long time, so she spent hours observing wildlife, and understanding the amazing lives of many insects. Today, her paintings help scientists understand how the wildlife in Suriname is adapting to climate change. Maria shows that anyone can be a scientist—all we need to do is look a bit closer at the world around us!

FUN FACT

Maria's paintings are now found in museums and galleries across the world, and you can still buy her books!

John Harrison
Making time

For thousands of years, humans have used boats to sail across oceans. The ancient Egyptians, Greeks, and Polynesians set sail to discover new lands, and for trade. By the 1600s, many European countries had also taken to the seas. But sailors often got lost, without an accurate way to figure out where exactly they were...

Lost at sea

Early explorers drew maps of their travels, dividing the world into a grid. Horizontal lines of latitude told them how far north or south they were, and vertical lines of longitude told them how far east or west they were. These maps showed sailors where they were setting off from and heading to, and any dangers on the way. They couldn't, however, tell them one key thing: where on the map they were at a specific time.

Sailors could figure out their latitude by measuring where the sun was in the sky at midday. Figuring out their longitude was also easy—in theory. All they needed to know was what time the sun rose. It rises earlier in the east, so knowing the time of sunrise would tell them where in the world they were. This only worked with an accurate measurement, though; if their clock was a minute slow, it could put them 17 miles off course! The problem was, accurate clocks did not exist yet, so sailors often got lost.

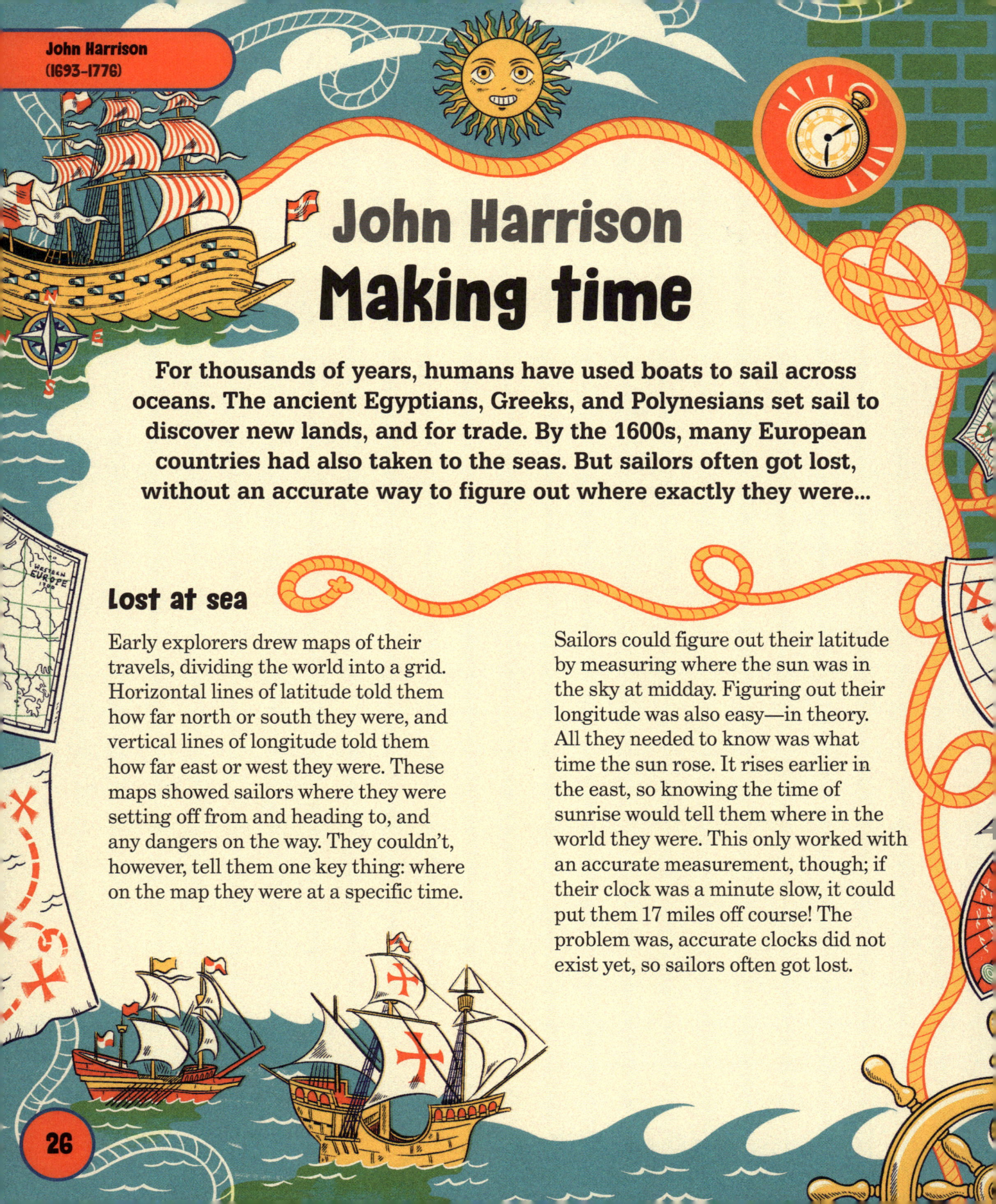

The Longitude Prize

£1,500,000

FUN FACT
Accurate clocks were used for navigation until the 1970s, when the first GPS satellites were launched. These gave ships their exact longitude and latitude.

Time for a change

The British Government realized things needed to change. They set up The Longitude Prize, offering the equivalent of £1.5 million to anyone who could design an accurate clock. Clocks at this time were mechanical objects. A pendulum would rotate cogs and gears and move the clock hands. These pendulums did not work well on swaying ships, which is why it was so hard to measure the time at sea.

This prize caught the attention of young carpenter John Harrison, who had loved clocks since childhood. He taught himself to build clocks in his spare time, without a formal education.

27

A clock fit for a king

John immediately started to work, but took 45 years to come up with a design he felt was good enough. This clock could fit in the palm of a hand, and used a coiled spring instead of a pendulum. It worked perfectly, too, losing only 5 seconds after 81 days at sea. The judge of the competition, however, refused to give John the prize. Why? He was trying to win too! John complained directly to the king and finally, at the age of 80, he was given the full prize.

FUN FACT

By 1860, the British Navy had less than 200 ships, but over 800 chronometers (marine clocks)!

Taking your time

John Harrison spent his whole life doing what he loved most: designing and building clocks. But he also used this passion to change the world, helping avoid hundreds of shipwrecks and saving thousands of lives in the process.

John Harrison's four original chronometers are on display at the Royal Observatory in London.

FUN FACT

John's final design even had an alarm bell that rang to remind sailors to wind its spring back up and keep it powered.

Michael Faraday
The pioneer of electricity

Michael Faraday made many discoveries that our modern technology-filled world relies on, but many people have never heard of him! This is because he was not interested in awards or recognition. Instead, he enjoyed being in his lab, working away at problems, and changing the world in the process.

From humble beginnings

Michael was born in a poor area of London, and would often have just a loaf of bread to eat for a whole week. He did not receive much education beyond learning to read and write.

Turning the page

By age 13, Michael needed to work to support his family. He delivered newspapers for a bookshop, and his hard work got him promoted to apprentice bookbinder, where he learned how to make books by hand. This was an amazing opportunity: he could read while he worked, helping him get the education he craved. He loved science books, especially those by Jane Marcet, one of the first prominent female science writers.

A customer saw his interest in science and gave him tickets to see some live lectures by chemist Humphry Davy, who was like a rock star at the time. These were filled with demonstrations, and were so popular that the street they took place on became the first one-way street in London in order to cope with the traffic!

A new world

Michael loved the lectures, and made it his goal to get a job at The Royal Institution, where he saw Humphry's lecture. He made his lecture notes into a beautiful book, which he sent to Humphry as a gift and job application! Luckily, a last-minute position came up, which Michael was very happy to fill.

One of his first jobs was to accompany Humphry on a tour of Europe. Michael had not traveled more than three miles outside of London before, so this was a fantastic experience. He marveled at the landscapes, climbing Mount Vesuvius in Italy, and even enjoying a meal cooked in its boiling volcanic waters! He also met some of the world's greatest scientists, filling his mind with inspiration and ideas.

FUN FACT

In Michael's time, labs used an usual piece of equipment: dead frogs! If the frog's legs twitched, it showed that electricity was flowing through a wire. Thankfully, a machine was eventually invented that could do this instead.

Humphry Davy

Electric discoveries

Michael spent most of his life working at The Royal Institution. He took detailed notes of all of his experiments, carefully developing each idea. His first invention was the electric motor, which spins inside everything from electric cars to smoothie makers. He also made a similar invention—the electric generator. This uses movement to create electricity, and is still how almost all electricity is generated today, from wind turbines to gas power stations.

Talking about science

Perhaps Michael's greatest work, however, was helping everyone understand science. He saw how important it was to help young people, just as Humphry Davy had done in his inspirational science talks. So he started the Christmas Lectures, a series of exciting demonstration-filled science talks. These lectures are still running today, almost 200 years after Michael started them.

FUN FACT

You are safe from lightning in an airplane or car thanks to another of Michael's inventions: the Faraday cage. This stops the energy from the lightning from getting inside. It is also used inside a microwave!

The modest Mr. Faraday

Expanding on his work with electricity, Michael also supported the British Government with improving its lighthouses, helping avoid shipwrecks just like John Harrison before him. Queen Victoria offered to give him a Knighthood and the title "Sir," to recognize his huge achievements. He declined this, however, stating that he wanted to remain as simply Mr. Faraday for the rest of his days.

MR. FARADAY'S CHRISTMAS LECTURE

33

Radhanath Sikdar
Mountains with math

Before computers, we relied on people to figure out difficult calculations. Radhanath Sikdar was an Indian mathematician employed by the government at just 19 years old. His boss quickly recognized his talent and he was given a very important job: measuring a mysterious new mountain, code-named "Peak 15."

Measuring with triangles

At this time, the Indian government was making accurate maps of the whole country. To measure distances, they used the mathematics of triangles. Imagine a huge triangle on the ground. If you know the length of one side, and the angles inside the triangle, you can use mathematics to figure out the length of the other two sides. Sikdar and his team could start with one accurately measured line, and build up a grid of triangles covering a large area of land.

The tallest peak

Sikdar and his team were not the first people to use math like this. Ancient Egyptian scribes like Imhotep used similar techniques to measure land and even build the pyramids! At the time, a mountain called Kangchenjunga in Bhutan was thought to be the tallest peak. Sikdar's boss thought "Peak 15" might be taller, so Sikdar was tasked with figuring out its height.

Using careful calculations, he measured "Peak 15" at exactly 29,000 ft (8,839.2 m). Sikdar was worried people might think this was just an estimated number, so he instead submitted his measurement as 29,002 ft. Many people, therefore, say that Sikdar was the first person to put two feet on this mountain, if only in his measurement!

A new name

Sikdar's measurement was accepted, and "Peak 15" was renamed Mount Everest, after his old boss, George Everest, even though he had never seen the mountain! Maybe it should be renamed "Mount Sikdar," to properly honor the pioneering mathematician whose careful calculations led to its recognition as the tallest peak in the world.

FUN FACT
Kangchenjunga is the world's third-highest mountain, but one of the hardest to climb. It is only 863 ft (263 m) shorter than Mount Everest.

Mount Everest is actually growing 0.15 in (4 mm) taller each year as it is being pushed up by movements of the Earth's crust.

Eunice Newton Foote
The first climate scientist

Since human activity exploded in the 1900s, the temperature of our planet has been rising, in a process called global warming. Amazingly, the cause of this warming, known as the greenhouse effect, was discovered by a scientist in her home lab over 150 years ago.

Science at home

Eunice Foote lived in the US, at a time when women's options were limited, and, compared to others, she was fortunate to get a full education. However, she was then expected to become a housewife. She got married, but she continued her education at home, experimenting in her own lab.

Windowsill experiments

At this time, scientists had just discovered earth was much warmer in the distant past, and magazines were filled with fantastical illustrations of the tropical swamps that once existed. This caught Eunice's attention, and in 1856 she devised an experiment to figure out the cause of this warming.

She filled one bottle with regular air, and one with carbon dioxide gas. She then left these in the sun. After a few hours, the regular air warmed to 100.4°F (38°C), but the carbon dioxide had shot up to 120.2°F (49°C)! She correctly concluded that if there was more carbon dioxide in our atmosphere, it would become warmer. Today, we call this the greenhouse effect.

FUN FACT
Eunice made many inventions in her time, including a cheaper way to make wrapping paper and a squeak-resistant shoe!

37

Rising up

Eunice's research was published, but didn't make much of an impact at the time. She carried on working in her home lab, making a number of successful inventions, which earned the family a comfortable income. She was also an early member of the Women's Rights Movement in the US, paving the way toward equal rights for women.

WOMEN'S RIGHTS CONVENTION

FUN FACT
Eunice's husband was a lawyer, so they patent-protected all of her inventions to stop people from illegally copying her ideas!

Double experiments

In 1859, an Irish scientist, John Tyndall, also discovered the greenhouse effect. Working in a professional lab, his equipment showed more detail about how the warming worked, and his fame helped his research spread. It is not clear if he knew of Eunice's work, but for most of history he was known as the person who discovered the greenhouse effect.

It was only in the 1990s that Eunice's contribution to climate science was rediscovered, and her pioneering work became known across the world.

Gregor Mendel
Growing knowledge

As well as studying how the world works, some scientists look at a smaller scale, such as the inside of an organism. One hugely important discovery, which reshaped our understanding of how all life works, occurred in an unlikely place—a cathedral in what is now the Czech Republic.

Countryside to cathedral

Gregor Mendel was born on his family farm in the countryside. From a young age, he helped his dad at work, learning to grow different fruits and vegetables. One day, his teacher suggested he study to be a monk at the local monastery. Gregor soon found a comfortable life there. The monastery had a large library of science books for him to read, and there was a garden where he could grow plants.

Trying to teach

As part of his work, Gregor became a trainee teacher at the local school. This took bravery because he was not comfortable talking in front of people. But he faced his fear and was a friendly and kind teacher. He eventually built up the courage to take the test to become a full-time teacher. But sadly, he never passed the exams.

28,000 plants

Gregor moved back to the monastery, and decided instead to spend his time peacefully working in the garden. He grew food, and investigated how plants grew. At this time, scientists understood that plants and animals inherited their characteristics from their parents, but how this actually happened was a mystery.

Gregor used peas for his experiments. He chose pea plants because they were easy to grow and had recognizable characteristics. The plants could be tall or short; and their peas could be green or yellow, and either wrinkly or smooth. He spent over eight years on this work, growing more than 28,000 plants!

FUN FACT

Scientists still study peas today. One research lab in the UK has over 3,500 different types of pea plants!

41

Just as Gregor observed his peas inheriting characteristics, humans can also inherit characteristics, including cheek dimples, freckles, and earlobes being attached or not attached to our heads!

Planting the seeds

Gregor mixed these different plants together, taking a plant with yellow peas and breeding it with one with green peas. He expected the offspring to have yellowy-green peas—a mix of the two parents.

This is not what happened, though, and the offspring were only green or yellow. Gregor made notes of his experiments, and saw that this happened with every characteristic he tried. He published his conclusions in 1865, but nobody paid much attention. He carried on with his life as a monk, eventually being put in charge of the whole monastery.

Slow fame

It was only in the 1950s that scientists realized how important Gregor's discovery was. By this time, we knew that organisms could adapt and change to suit their environments, passing on these changes to their offspring in a process called evolution. We also knew that this information was stored in a special molecule called DNA in our cells. Gregor's discovery linked this all together. His work showed that the different characteristics, such as yellow and green peas, were inherited by receiving a copy of DNA from each parent.

When he finished his work, Gregor said "Before long the entire world will praise the result of these labors." He was right—though it took almost 100 years!

FUN FACT
Gregor Mendel sent a copy of his research to Charles Darwin, who discovered evolution with Alfred Russel Wallace.

Alfred Russel Wallace
The other person of evolution

When it comes to the theory of evolution, people usually think of one person: Charles Darwin. But there was another scientist who independently developed the exact same idea at a similar time, and not a lot of people realize this!

A different upbringing

In the 1800s, almost all successful scientists came from families with money to pay for their education, and connections to help them get good jobs. Charles Darwin had the privilege of studying at Cambridge University, which then got him a job on a ship exploring South America. This voyage gave Charles the seeds of his theory of evolution—an idea he spent decades perfecting in the quiet of his country house.

Alfred Russel Wallace's start in life was different. His family struggled for money, forcing him to drop out of school at 14.

Alfred instead joined his brother as a surveyor. This sparked his passion for wildlife, and he spent his days walking through the countryside making maps and studying wildlife. However, being from a poor background, it was almost impossible for Alfred to share his research with established scientists.

When Charles returned from his voyage on his boat, he wrote a best-selling book about his travels. This gave Alfred a grand idea: he, too, would travel the world, making a name for himself as a scientist in the process.

A fateful first voyage

Alfred soon departed on his first trip, to explore the Rio Grande, a river flowing through the Amazon Rainforest. He planned to pay for this trip by collecting exotic animals and selling them when he returned home. Alfred collected many animals, and made the first accurate maps of the Rio Grande.

He was astounded by the diversity of life he saw on this trip. Sadly, on his journey back home, the ship carrying all his specimens caught fire. Most of Alfred's work sank to the bottom of the ocean.

A successful second attempt

Not deterred by his bad luck, Alfred quickly made plans for an even more ambitious voyage, to a large group of tropical islands in Southeast Asia. Even today, visitors would find traveling through these rainforests a challenge, so it is almost unimaginable that Alfred did this in the 1800s—in a thick woollen suit!

This trip was much more successful than his first, and he spent eight years collecting 126,000 specimens, including thousands of different species.

Many of these are still on display in museums across the world. However the trip nearly killed him; he caught malaria many times. It was while asleep with a fever deep in the jungle that Alfred had his breakthrough idea. He suddenly understood that the animal habitat patterns he had observed in the jungles were caused by species evolving and adapting to their environments.

A joint announcement

Alfred sent a letter explaining his theory to one of the best scientists he knew—Charles Darwin. Charles was shocked: he had just spent 20 years writing his theory of evolution, and Alfred had suddenly come up with the same idea! Their ideas were presented together to the scientific world in 1858. A year later Charles published his book *On the Origin of Species*, which explained the theory in more detail. This book was a bestseller, cementing Charles as the discoverer of evolution.

Evolution and our place in the world

Although Alfred was never as well known as Charles, he continued his work as a scientist, studying the natural world. Alfred's work shows us that we are just a small part of the amazing complexity of life on Earth, and we need to do our best to preserve it in any way that we can.

FUN FACT
Alfred is a hero to many scientists today, and over 300 new species have been named after him!

Granville T. Woods
The power of invention

In the mid-1800s, the world was changing fast, with inventors creating amazing new things and transforming lives. Working at this time were famous inventors like Thomas Edison, one of the inventors of the light bulb, and Nikola Tesla, a master of electrical experimentation.

Getting hands-on

Life was very hard for Black Americans. Slavery had only just been banned, and many still faced discrimination and hate, making it difficult to find a job or succeed in life. Granville T. Woods grew up in this world. He was only in school until he was 10, and after this he worked as an apprentice in a variety of hands-on jobs. He learned to melt and shape metal as a blacksmith, how to build and fix trains, and how to lay down train tracks.

Alongside this, Granville read as much as he could. He'd often get friends to borrow books for him because many libraries did not allow Black people inside. He loved to read about electricity, and soon realized that this was the future.

An electric start

As a young man, Granville decided to become an inventor himself, inspired by the world of electricity he had read about. There are two ways to make money as an inventor: by building your own inventions, or by selling your ideas to a company.

One of Granville's first inventions was a better version of the telephone, which had recently been invented by Alexander Graham Bell. Alexander quickly saw the genius in Granville's invention and paid him a large sum of money to buy it. This finally gave Granville the funds he needed to become a full-time inventor.

Granville tested his ideas for electric trains by making the first electric roller-coaster, at Coney Island, New York.

Back on track

Granville had spent a lot of his teenage years working on railroads across the country. This was a dangerous place, with trains often crashing into each other. The main problem was that trains had no way to communicate with each other, or with train stations. A train could be speeding down the tracks with no idea another train was broken down just around the corner.

Granville solved this problem. Using ideas first explored by Michael Faraday, he created a way for trains to send messages along the telephone wires next to the tracks. This helped avoid hundreds of accidents, saving thousands of lives.

Beating the competition

Granville's amazing invention caught the attention of Thomas Edison, the most famous inventor in the US. Jealous of his success, he took Granville to court, accusing him of stealing this idea. Granville easily proved the idea was his own and won. Thomas then tried to use his money to win, offering Granville a well-paid job in his company. Granville refused the offer, knowing he was smarter than Thomas and better off working alone.

Granville would go on to make over 60 inventions in his lifetime, some of which are still used today. He had to fight for his work all his life, with Thomas taking him to court a second time, and another business partner stealing his drawings. Although he is not well known today, any time you take a train, you are safe thanks to his pioneering work.

FUN FACT

Granville designed a safety braking system for trains that is still used today. It automatically applies the brakes if the driver falls unconscious.

FUN FACT

To stop people from copying your ideas, you can apply for patents. These record your designs with the government, showing that you invented them, and means people can only use the ideas if you agree.

Henrietta Swan Leavitt
Reaching for the stars

People have always looked up at the night sky, trying to make sense of the vast expanse of stars. Our understanding has changed drastically over time, though. Many ancient cultures thought the night sky was a great flat roof above earth. It took the hard work of an astronomer to show the true, vast size of our universe.

An education of firsts

Henrietta Swan Leavitt was born in a time of change. Her school was the first in the US to teach boys and girls together, and she was one of the first women to study at a university, too. This gave her the chance to learn about many subjects, including English, music, philosophy, and math.

She especially enjoyed astronomy, and after her studies, she offered to work at the university observatory for free. She was eventually given a paid role, but her opportunities were limited by being a woman. She worked as a human computer, like Radhanath Sikdar, doing the repetitive, detailed calculations that her male colleagues didn't want to do.

Henrietta identified 1,777 new variable stars in the course of her work.

Maximum brightness of stars

Star brightness

12
13
14
15
16

0.0 0.2 0.4 0.6 0.8 1.0 1.2 1.4 1.6 1.8 2.0 2.2

Minimum brightness of stars

Time between flashes

A stellar discovery

Henrietta was given the job of studying variable stars—newly discovered stars that slowly flashed between light and dim. She was not allowed to use the telescope—that was deemed to be a man's job—so she instead carefully studied photographs taken over the last ten years. This was painstaking work. She had to find the same stars on photographs taken at different times, and measure how bright they were. She did these measurements for hundreds of thousands of photographs during her career.

By carefully studying thousands of different stars, Henrietta made a world-changing discovery: by measuring how bright a variable star was, and how fast it flashed, she realized you could figure out how far away it was. She had come up with the first way to measure the size of the universe, without ever touching a telescope!

A computer's life

As a "computer," Henrietta had no choice which projects she worked on. Her boss published her groundbreaking work under his name, and she was moved on to other projects. She spent the rest of her working life at the observatory, in an all-female team of computers who discovered thousands of stars and galaxies in their time.

A decade after her work was published, another astronomer, Edwin Hubble, used Henrietta's ideas to measure the size of the universe and, more controversially, show that it is in fact still growing larger. It was only in 2008 that Henrietta's amazing work was properly recognized, when astronomers formally named her discovery "Leavitt's Law."

FUN FACT

A telescope in the US has been named after Henrietta—part of a network of telescopes across the world that automatically scan the entire night sky in one day.

An asteroid was named after Henrietta, which orbits the sun once every five years.

Inge Lehmann
Amazing to the core

Like Henrietta Swan Leavitt, Inge Lehmann went to a school that educated both girls and boys. Inge lived in Denmark and was free to pursue her love of math and science. She studied math at a university and then became an actuary, which meant she used her mathematical skills to help solve a wide range of problems.

Earthshaking discovery

Inge found her real passion in life by accident, when she worked as an assistant to a professor of seismology—the study of earthquakes. Thousands of earthquakes happen every year, and research stations across the world measure the waves of energy they create. Inge used her mathematical mind to explore this mountain of information for patterns.

What she saw didn't make sense. At the time, scientists thought Earth was a ball of liquid rock with a thin solid layer on top. The data showed Inge that earthquake energy waves were bouncing off something inside the earth. She had discovered earth's core! Her data showed that earth actually has two layers of solid and liquid metal at the center, surrounded by molten rock. This changed how scientists understood our planet's structure.

FUN FACT
Inge kept all her earthquake measurements on small cards, stored in cereal boxes.

A well-earned break

Inge was deservedly well recognized for this discovery. She received awards from around the world and spent the rest of her career studying earthquakes. Her colleagues described her as an expert at looking through information and finding hidden patterns that even a modern computer would not be able to find.

Inge died at the amazing age of 104, making her one of the longest-lived female scientists.

57

Percy Julian
Powered by plants

For thousands of years, people have used plants for medicine. Extracting compounds directly from plants is expensive, and chemists look for alternative methods. Percy Julian was one of the pioneers of this. His achievements are even more impressive considering the barriers he faced as a Black scientist in the United States.

Working through barriers

When Percy Julian was young, Black and white students were sent to separate schools. Schools for Black children were given limited resources, but despite this, Percy made it to college and finished at the top of his class. He then taught at a university, before studying plant chemistry in Austria.

Upon returning to the US, Percy took a job at a paint factory. It was not the role he wanted, but it was the only way he could work as a chemist.

An accidental breakthrough

One day, a colleague reported water leaking onto the plant oils they used in their paints. Percy observed a white solid forming. He took this to his lab to analyze and was astounded—this chemical was similar to many chemicals in our body! He soon turned this accident into a business.

Percy set up his own company, producing cheaper medicines from plants. He later sold the company for the equivalent of $21 million, using this money to support a range of charities. Although he had to work against many barriers in his life, Percy Julian achieved amazing things, and his discoveries are still used in medicines to this day.

Quinine, an important drug used to treat malaria, is only found in the bark of a tropical tree from South America.

FUN FACT
Percy had over 100 patents for the medicines he invented in his lifetime.

Rachel Carson
A silent hero

By the 1900s, scientists across the world had made huge technological achievements, but little thought had been given to how our natural environment could cope with this rapid development. We owe much of our understanding of the impact humans have on the environment to the brave work of Rachel Carson.

An ocean of potential

Rachel grew up on a farm in the countryside in Pennsylvania, and spent her childhood exploring the forests and rivers.

She enjoyed English at school, and went to college to study it, but her love of nature caused her to switch to biology. Rachel then found a paid job working for the government wildlife service. Fortunately, her job helped her combine her passion for nature with writing—she made radio programs and magazine articles to help the public understand the amazing wildlife in oceans and rivers.

Rachel wrote three popular books about the ocean. Unlike other science authors at the time, she used her love of poetry and novels to write scientific stories. This made her books easy to read, and very popular. These books brought in enough money for Rachel to become a full-time author.

Rachel's first radio program was called "Romance Under the Waters." It featured stories of the amazing animals found in oceans and rivers.

Rachel's boss thought her writing was "too good for the government" and encouraged her to write books instead.

Silent spring

Meanwhile, the use of chemicals to kill insects and other farm pests was becoming common around the world. Chemicals helped farmers grow more food, but the impact they had on the environment was unclear. A new chemical, called DDT, was capable of killing hundreds of insect species at once. Rachel's friend wrote to her in alarm, describing birds dying in the thousands after nearby farms were treated with DDT. This was a wake-up call for Rachel, who devoted the next four years to researching pesticides.

She wrote about her work in a book called *Silent Spring*. The title was chosen to represent what the world would be like with continued DDT use—no insects, no birds, no animals; just silence.

Truth is power

Silent Spring described the damage caused by DDT and other pesticides. Not only did they kill insects, but also the animals that ate these insects. Rachel explained this complicated information clearly, showing that the species with which we share the planet were vulnerable to human activity.

Rachel's book caused a storm as soon as it was published. Companies that produced pesticides attempted to discredit her. Some even published their own stories, describing a famine-filled world that was the result of not having their "amazing" products. Thankfully, the truth in *Silent Spring* was impossible to argue with, and eventually DDT was banned.

The first environmentalist

Rachel changed how people thought about the planet. She showed that human activity and progress can often be at the expense of the natural world. Although she sadly died before she could see the impact of her work, young people, like Greta Thunberg, are continuing her legacy and making sure we preserve the planet for the generations to come.

Hedy Lamarr
The Hollywood inventor

When you sit down to watch a movie, you are likely amazed by the sights and sounds, and blown away by the acting. But did you know that there might be a scientist hiding in plain view? Hedy Lamarr was one of the most popular actresses in the golden age of Hollywood, but she was also an inventor whose work still impacts our lives today.

Science takes the stage

Hedy Lamarr grew up in Austria and trained to be an actress. But she was also interested in science, taking apart radios in her bedroom and quizzing her dad on technology. As a young woman, she moved to the United States to pursue her acting career.

Hedy quickly became a hit, acting in many of the greatest films of the 1940s. But she never forgot her passion for science. She even had a workshop built so she could work on her inventions during breaks in filming.

The secret scientist

As World War II raged on, Hedy felt frustrated with her comfortable life. So she decided to put her scientific mind to work. She helped a friend design faster airplanes, taking inspiration from birds, just like Abbas ibn Firnas over a thousand years before.

Her greatest invention was a method of secret communication. Working with a musician friend, she invented a radio system to send messages. This hopped between 88 radio channels, making it impossible to hack. Why 88? Because that's the number of keys on a piano!

Many of her inventions were classified as secret, and few of her fellow actors knew she had a hidden life as an inventor.

Inspiring the future

Hedy Lamarr felt people judged her by her looks, thinking she was simply an attractive actress. Her legacy proves otherwise, with her work still impacting the world today. Any wireless device using Bluetooth technology is based on her work— a pretty big impact, considering there are over 10 billion Bluetooth devices in the world!

FUN FACT
Hedy Lamarr invented a tablet that could dissolve into water, transforming it into a fizzy drink like cola!

Marie Tharp
An oceanic discovery

In the 1900s, maps of the world were highly detailed, until they got to oceans, which were simply shown as a flat, blue expanse. It took the pioneering work of Marie Tharp to uncover the amazing complexity of the sea floor—all without being allowed to step foot on a ship.

Map-making

Marie Tharp spent her childhood on the move, traveling across the US with her family. Her dad worked as a soil surveyor, taking measurements of the ground and making maps. Marie often helped her dad at work, giving her an early love of geology.

Marie studied English, art, and math in college because geology was seen as a subject only for men. But, when men went to help in World War II in the 1940s, she was accepted to study geology. She was, however, restricted to the office, working with data that her male colleagues collected out in the field.

At the start of the 1900s, a scientist named Alfred Wegener suggested a revolutionary idea—that the surface of the earth was made up of moving plates, which formed mountains when they collided, and new land when they moved apart. This idea was dismissed as impossible at the time, with little evidence supporting Alfred's idea.

Mapping the invisible

Marie's first job as a geologist was making maps of the ocean floor. She made these using something unusual—sound. Ships would send pings down to the ocean floor, and listen for when an echo bounced back. The time this took would tell Marie how deep the ocean was at that spot.

As Marie transformed this abstract data into a visual map, she noticed something astounding. The ocean floor was not flat, but amazingly complex, filled with mountains and valleys.

Seeing is believing

One feature in particular caught Marie's eye. There was a 10,000 mile (16,000 km) long underwater mountain ridge with a deep valley at its center. She knew at once what she was looking at—a place where two plates were moving apart. She had found the first evidence to support Alfred's theory!

Her colleagues weren't convinced, however, dismissing her ideas. Marie later showed them earthquakes occurring in the same location on the map as these ridges, caused by plates moving apart. But still people didn't believe her, with ocean explorer Jacques Cousteau paying for a costly expedition to photograph the ocean floor and disprove her. His photos instead showed exactly what Marie Tharp's maps predicted!

Marie only stepped foot on a research ship in 1968, long after her world-changing maps were first published.

A whole new world

By 1977, Marie had mapped all of the world's oceans. These amazing maps completely revolutionized the world of geology, showing the complex landscape hidden between the waves, and providing the first evidence that plates move.

Despite the fact that her contributions were overlooked for much of her life, Marie was confident in what she achieved. She described her work as a "once in the history of the world" opportunity.

Fazlur Khan
Building to the skies

Although the pyramids built by Imhotep are impressive, there are even taller skyscrapers towering over our cities today. But these buildings are possible thanks to the creative ideas of Fazlur Khan, who used nature to build tall.

Bangladesh and bamboo

Fazlur Khan grew up in what is now Bangladesh, surrounded by forests of bamboo plants towering over the local houses. Fazlur studied engineering in college, with his talents earning him a fully paid place to continue studying in the US.

Tall and cheap

Fazlur Khan grew up at the dawn of the skyscraper. These giants could rise so high thanks to a stiff and heavy steel frame. The Empire State Building, for example, has 210 steel columns on each floor! This makes for a heavy, but also expensive, building.

Fazlur soon started to design tall buildings himself. A customer came to him one day, asking whether he could build them a 90-story skyscraper for $100 million. "No," he replied. "With $100 million, we can build a 100-story skyscraper."

Inspired by nature

To design these colossal buildings for less money required a revolutionary new design. Fazlur planned the exterior of the skyscraper as a steel shell, just like the hollow bamboo he saw growing as a child. This tubular structure made the skyscraper strong, but used half as much steel as other skyscrapers.

In 1973, he used this method to build the world's then tallest building, the Sears Tower (now the Willis Tower), joining nine of these tubes together in a super-strong bundle.

A whole new world

Fazlur's tubular designs were much better at dealing with strong winds, allowing skyscrapers to be built higher and higher. Even today, anyone starting to structure a tall building starts with his revolutionary design.

FUN FACT

The Sears (Willis) Tower was the tallest tower in the world for over 20 years.

Gladys West
A new way to navigate

In 1957, a huge milestone happened: the first satellite was launched into space. Today, satellites are crucial to modern life, with a common use being navigation, or GPS. This simple tool relies on some surprisingly complex math from the amazing mind of Gladys West.

Away from the farm

Gladys West grew up on a farm in Virginia. She loved school and wanted to go to college, but her family could not afford it. Thankfully, Gladys found a chance. If she got the highest test results in her state, the government would pay for her studies. Gladys did it! She took mathematics and wasn't discouraged by the fact there were mostly white men in her classes. Money was still tight, so she became a teacher before continuing her studies.

The age of computers

After graduating, Gladys became a mathematician for the US Navy, one of only two Black women working for them at the time. This was a period of huge change. The first computers had arrived and were transforming the world. They were capable of running calculations faster than even amazing mathematicians like Gladys.

One of the first projects Gladys and her team used the computer for was accurately plotting the movements of Pluto and Neptune. These calculations took the computer over 100 hours!

Measuring the Earth

By the 1970s, satellites had become more advanced, and could monitor things like earth's temperature. A huge goal was to use networks of satellites for navigation. For this to work, satellites needed to know how far they were from the earth. This was not easy because the earth is not a perfect sphere. Gladys was the one who solved this problem. She wrote programs for the computer and made a 3D model of the earth. Her model was a key part of satellite navigation, and is still used today.

FUN FACT

The early computers Gladys used were the fastest in the world, but a modern phone can do calculations 70,000 times faster.

A scientist to the end

Gladys continued her work on satellites until she was 68. However, her journey as a scientist wasn't done yet. She then went back to college, only retiring at the age of 70. Gladys worked hard her whole life, showing that people can achieve their goals and change the world for the better.

You!
Future scientist

So many amazing scientists have helped make the world we enjoy today possible—far too many to fit them all in this book! But what about the future? Who will carry on the work done by the amazing scientists you've met so far? Why not you?

Hopefully you've seen that anyone in the world can be a scientist if they want to be. Who in this book inspired you the most? What might you like to achieve when you are older?

Here are some skills that you will find useful if you want to be a scientist:

 **Passion**
Most of the scientists you met in this book loved doing science!
Find a subject you really enjoy, and get exploring.

 **Creativity**
Science isn't about just learning things from a book. You need to come up with new ideas, different ways to experiment, or entirely new theories. The only limit is your imagination!

 **Determination**
Doing science isn't always easy, and things don't always happen the way you want them to. An important skill as a scientist is to keep going. Always work hard toward your goals and don't let failure stop you.

 **Caring**
Science is a great way for us to help people and the planet. How might you be able to use your scientific skills to help a good cause?

Go beyond science
Scientists don't just need to be good at science! Language skills help you communicate your ideas, and art helps you showcase them visually.

Wherever the world of science goes next will be completely up to the work of amazing people across the world, which might include you!

GLOSSARY

abstract existing as an idea or thought, but without a physical existence

actuary a person employed by insurance companies to figure out how much they should charge their clients for insurance

analyze to examine something, often using scientific methods, in order to fully understand it

apprentice a beginner who works for someone and is learning their skill

asteroid a small, rocky object that orbits the sun

astronomy the study of space

blacksmith someone who makes and repairs things from iron by hand

Bluetooth a technology that allows devices to communicate with each other without wires

civilization a society where people have built a complex city or country

complexity the state of being intricate or complicated

compounds substances that consist of two or more elements

demigod a mythological being who is part mortal, part god

deterred discouraged or prevented

discrimination treating a group of people unfairly because of their characteristics or beliefs, for example their gender, race, or religion

engineering designing and constructing engines and machinery, or structures such as bridges

environmentalist a person who is concerned with protecting and preserving the natural environment

geology the study of the earth's structure, surface, and origins

harmonious tuneful; well-matched

inherit to be born with a quality or characteristic your parents or ancestors also had

innovative new and original

lavish luxurious or elaborate

legacy the long-lasting impact of events or a person's life

malaria a serious disease carried by mosquitoes, which causes high fever

molten rock rock that has been heated to a very high temperature and has become a liquid

monastery a building or buildings occupied by a community of monks living under religious vows

observatory a building with a large telescope, from which astronomers study the night sky

offspring the children or young of an animal or plant

organism any living thing

painstaking extremely careful and thorough

pendulum a weight hung from a fixed point so that it can swing freely

pesticides chemicals that farmers use to control pests

pioneer a person who is one of the first to explore a new place

preserve to keep something in its current state, so that it does not change or end

prominent important, famous, or noticeable

propelling driving or pushing something forward

pupae insects that are between larvae and adults, sometimes wrapped inside chrysalises or cocoons

revolutionary causing a complete or dramatic change

satellite any object that orbits a planet or sun, but often a machine that collects scientific information

specimens plants or animals that are used or studied by scientists, as examples of a particular species or type

surveyor a person who examines the condition of land and buildings

theory a formal idea or system of ideas that is intended to explain something

tubular long, round, and hollow, like a tube

Index

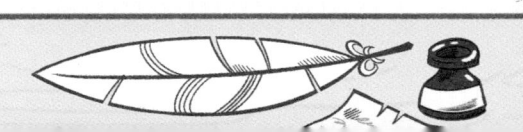

About the Royal Institution

The Royal Institution is an independent science education charity based in London, UK. It was founded in 1799 with a clear vision: to be a place where anyone could come to enjoy learning about science and the world around us.

Many amazing people have worked here over the last 200+ years, including Michael Faraday, who you have already met. In fact, scientists who worked at the Royal Institution have discovered or isolated 10 elements of the periodic table and won an amazing 15 Nobel Prizes! Today we spend our time running exciting activities, to help people of all ages discover the wonders of science. Maybe you have seen our Christmas Lectures online? These are science lectures, for young people just like you, broadcast on TV every year and available on YouTube. We also run events all year long, from explosion-packed Theatre talks to interactive science workshops. We travel to schools all across the UK too. Here at the Royal Institution, we believe that science is for everyone, especially you!

Hello from the author

Hi there, I'm Peter and I really hope you enjoyed reading this book! Since childhood, I have always loved learning about science and exploring nature, whether it was reading my animal atlas, or simply exploring in the woods. As an adult I have carried on with this passion.

First, I studied Zoology at the University of Sheffield, before living in the Alps in Switzerland, showing young people the amazing nature and wildlife there. I am excited to now be working with the Royal Institution, writing books for budding scientists just like you!